What's in Your House?

Arifah N. Goodwin

What's in Your House?

For more information, address Arifah Goodwin via:

Email: *ArifahGoodwinEmpowers@gmail.com*

Website: www.GoodEmpowers.com

First Printing, 2019

ISBN: 9781798066522

Table of Contents

Acknowledgments and Dedication..1

Introduction 2

Chapter 1: Established in 1972..4

Chapter 2: He Knows My Name 8

Chapter 3: The Dreamer in Me...17

Chapter 4: Grateful Soles to Souls...25

Chapter 5: What's in Your House?..39

Chapter 6: You Hold The Keys!..51

Chapter 7: Strong Bonds...67

Chapter 8: Living Under Grace..77

Special Bonus: Journal Writing Prompts.......................................83

Acknowledgments and Dedication

God is my source and strength and I'd like to thank Him for the gift of life and salvation. I also wish to thank my wonderful husband who showed me how to laugh again. He supports my dreams and so effortlessly encourages me to be all that I am created to be. To my daughters, you are and will forever be my reasons. Our bond is deep and unbreakable.

I dedicate this book to all the beautiful women who God has allowed me to encounter. He so strategically created a space and time for each of them to have a major impact in my life. Whether you were aware or not, I thank you for being examples of what it means to embody a woman of purpose.

Introduction

It is no secret that for centuries, women are indoctrinated since little girls to believe that having success means striving for and obtaining the husband, the children, the nice car, the money, a big house and white picket fence. The Barbie and Ken ideology gives many the impression that once you have that life, come hell or high water, you quietly do and accept whatever you have to keep it. Many of us were led to believe that this was the autonomy of happiness, along with smiling all the time, whether you're happy or not and staying thin.

In a perfect world, this would be ideal, but it voids the reality of the day-to-day challenges, the pit stops, the barriers, roadblocks and obstacles that are bound to come and what makes this life so perfectly imperfect. What I grew to understand is that it's not about perfection but the fact that life was built and strategically constructed to strengthen and develop imperfect people.

Over the years, I have been that woman. I have had the opportunity to minister to women who were desperately seeking a deeper understanding of who they were, could be, desired to be and supposed to be without knowing what avenues to take to obtain it. This is especially difficult after being knocked down and told "no" so many times. You can start to forget what it sounds like to hear a "yes". Life challenges can really take a toll on a woman physically, mentally and spiritually if she does not know what is inside of her.

"What's in Your House" represents the power of God living and moving in us every single day we take a breath. What is challenging is that many of us have not discovered it or do not know how to activate it so it can work on our behalf. It's a beautiful thing to know that God has already set the foundation, brick by brick, wall by wall and strategically opens doors so all we really have to do is tap on the door to see what's inside.

In writing this book, I was inspired to share my personal experiences and the many lessons that life has tried to teach me over the years in order to sustain me and overcome some difficult and challenging times in my life. I hope that my story uplifts, empowers and challenges you to move forward in your life in a positive way, believing boldly that your pain is purposeful. Your life is full of promise and you can persevere! It is my prayer that you receive divine insight from God as you read about my experiences while evaluating your own. I pray more than anything that a brand new relationship between you and God is formed like you've never imagined!

Chapter 1

Established in 1972

"Once we are destined to live out our lives in the prison of our own mind, it is our duty to furnish it well." ~ Peter Ustinov

Through wisdom, a house is built, and by understanding it is established; by knowledge the rooms are filled with all precious and pleasant riches. ~ Proverbs 24:3-4

I've always had a real curious spirit. I asked tons of questions and wanted to know how everything worked. I was the child that was sent out of the room because I constantly tried to be in "grown folks'" business. I was the "why" child; the child that grown folks called wise beyond their years and looked at as having an "old soul" as the elders would lovingly say.

In the year of 1972, so many fascinating things had taken place in the world. The first black female presidential candidate, Shirley Chisholm and Barbara Jordan became the first African-Americans to win House seats. Maya Angelou, a famed poet, produced and premiered the motion picture, "Georgia". She became the first black woman ever to accomplish this feat. Then came me. I was born on December 31, 1972.

What was I going to do great? Would it be enough for someone to one day talk and write about it? Being born on the last day of the year for a long time made me feel like I was an afterthought by God. I pictured us standing in line to be born and He chose his best picks first. When He got to me, He looked around and said, "Come on, girl. Let's go!" That's how I made the cut. For years, I joked about my late arrival into this world. Though I may have joked about being an afterthought, it was not so. In fact, I would learn just how serious God is about His children and my arrival date was intentional.

The book that I've grown to love and live by over the years told me that He knew me before I was even shaped and formed in my mother's womb. He knew me before there was a hair on my head or skin on my body. I don't know of anyone in my life that has ever given thought of me in such a detailed way.

My mother shared with me when I was much older how she often thinks back on when her doctor told her that she really should have had an abortion with me because she was so young and just had my brother a few years prior. If she had made that decision, I would not have had all those life's deaths that were swallowed up in victory. I wouldn't have learned how to survive and triumph through the storms that were to come. I wouldn't truly understand that my life had a purpose from the start of 1972 till this day. I wouldn't have lived to know that even through my lifetime, the devil would visit me regularly to remind me about how angry he was that my mother didn't cut my life short. He would tell me that I was still an afterthought by God. I didn't understand why the devil didn't like me so much. Why on earth would he pick on a child? Why would he consume my mind with so many negative thoughts at such a young age? I didn't know that from the year 1972 until now I would spend so much time fighting him just to keep my mind.

What I've learned about the devil is that he has an early recruitment program. He knew that if he could take complete control over the way I saw myself as a child, by the time I hit my teens, I would have self-destructed. However, the devil didn't prepare for God to do all that shaping and forming me before it was time for me to reach the womb.

He placed something inside of me that wasn't even made known to me. I had something within me so strong that it would act as my protection when the enemy tried over and over again to destroy my inner being. It would be my guide when the devil tried and did lead me astray. It would be my voice when the world tried to silence me and my love when it physically walked away. In 1972, I was born but I often refer to my date of my birth as a house being built. God wrote, on my foundation, that though I would take up residence of the house I would still belong to Him. I was built in 1972 but it would take a lifetime to discover all of the rooms in my house. It would take time to discover the doors that would both open and shut in my face and the height of the ceilings as I looked up at them with sometimes swollen eyes from tears that would fall over and over again. The floors and the windows would be mysteries. Lastly, that dark basement. If you've ever been in a dark place, you know that basements could get pretty dark and lonely.

God constructed our houses but He gives us the free will to invite guests. Sistah, we must be real careful with who and what we allow to take up residence. If we don't, the things we allow inside may not always leave so willingly. It's our duty to protect what God established and furnish it well so that we can live a life that will impact everything around us. I would discover, that just like the strong powerful women that made their mark on the world in 1972, it is now my responsibility to make the mark for God's glory and to impact someone else.

Chapter 2

He Knows My Name

My name was legally changed when I was around 11 years old from Antoinette Michelle Jones to Arifah Najah Muhammad. My parents are Muslim and the changing of our names was important to them. They decided to make the change over the summer to transition my brother and I. I can still recall the day when they told us that our names were changed. There wasn't some long drawn out discussion about it. It happened and it was final. I'm sure they had discussed it in length and came to the conclusion that based on their Islamic faith, this was best for the family.

I don't know if it was the changing of the names that was most difficult to absorb or the adjustment others would have to make when interacting with me. Maybe both? Who was I now? I left at the end of one school year as Antoinette Michelle Jones and returned Arifah Najah Muhammad. Who in the world was she? I didn't even like how the name sounded! I dreaded that first day back to school because, at some point, the teacher would have to call my name. I struggled all summer getting used to it but now, I found myself back around my peers who were too young to have the wisdom or understanding of my new reality. Some kids who were once our friends thought we were now the "weird kids". They didn't understand or knew any other kids that had their first name changed. I became a target for abuse and it came strong.

I can't tell you the amount of bullying that we endured. No matter how much I tried to write my name out on a piece of paper so that I could get used to saying and writing it, I just couldn't relate it to myself. I wasn't even sure if I was supposed to act like an Arifah. What in the world did that look like? After a while, my parent's saw how hard it had become to adjust to our new names. This pushed them to try a different approach of educating us on what our names meant. My parents explained to me that my first name meant "knowing and aware of," and my middle name meant "success." Looking back on this, I now see how much of an impact this decision affected me and my identity. My parents saw the importance of not focusing on the name itself but the meaning of the name and how we should live up to the meaning. They focused on what they hoped for in us and set a standard that reflected that standard. Looking back, it amazes me how much their decision was very Christ-like.

When God changed a person's name and gave him a new one, it was usually to establish a new identity. God changed Abram's name, meaning "high father," to "Abraham," meaning "father of a multitude" (Genesis 17:5). At the same time, God changed Abraham's wife's name from "Sarai," meaning "my princess," to "Sarah," meaning "mother of nations" (Genesis 17:15) and God changed Jacob's name, which meant "supplanter," to "Israel," meaning "having power with God" (Genesis 32:28). I see now that a name change is God's way of transforming you into something better while giving you something to aspire to.

"Knowing and aware of" and this new middle name, meaning "Success." It was one thing to adapt to the names but now added pressure was given to live up to the name. In my mind, it set a precedent that I couldn't fail. I had to be perfect and that I'd better have some sense in my head. I had to do something worthwhile in this world or I would be a letdown to everyone.

However, my reality was that I had no idea how to be anything like that. Although I liked school, was called wise beyond my years by my elders, and much smarter than I would allow on paper, I constantly got into trouble for having a sweet face and a smart mouth. If anything, I had succeeded in being the best eye roller in all of Dinwiddie, Virginia. I just didn't see myself at all as these names described. I went from this new identity to having an identity crisis!

The pressure I put on myself to progress at high performance took on a life of labels, titles, and a slew of unrealistic expectations that would not only affect me but those around me. Little did I know that this would be a battle I'd fight for years to come. The idea that you must reach a certain place before you experience real success voids the wisdom that's needed to put things into proper perspective. For me, it resulted in people-pleasing behaviors, never wanting to be wrong and terrified of failure. So many times, it was my immaturity that spoke up for me and said, I couldn't be wrong about anything. The spirit of pride is a dangerous thing but life would teach me over and over that the more I failed to die to pride, the more I would have to go through some of the same tests and trials over and over again.

Have you ever had to take a test over when you knew you were not prepared and you failed again? The teacher allowed you another chance to take it again and once again, with your unprepared self, failed. But the committed teacher, who believed in you, gave you another chance because this time knew you would do what it took to pass. Once again, you failed to study because you didn't see the need. Even after you've been given the study guide, the pencil, and the scantron, you failed again. We can compare this to our relationship with God. God, with all of His patience toward us, has issued out many tests in hopes that we would just pass this time. After failed attempts at the tests, He would teach me that I didn't have to learn the same lessons over again if I'd just listen to His instructions the first time. Whew! This itself would be an ongoing lesson but I am thankful there are no final exams with God. He's just merciful enough to let us try again.

As the lessons build brick by brick, the foundation of my perspective on things became more settled. I was able to have a greater appreciation for that one terrifying word, "failure". When God gives you a new identity, He starts to shift your self-perception into something more purposeful. You must know that if you do not think differently about who you are, you'll always live in the shadow of your former self. You'll never embrace who you are, where you currently are or where you are headed. Your perspective must change.

Often times, people remain the same because they are afraid of failure. Being afraid of failing will leave you comfortable and stuck in the same place for years. There is a solution.

I decided to make failure a friend. God changed my perspective on what it meant to experience it and how I saw myself after the experience. Even the things I had thought I heard God on, I prayed for, put my faith to work and believed that it would come to pass and it still didn't give me the desired outcome. I used to fall apart, which made the recovery time much longer than what it needed to be. Through the Word, God began to explain timing to me. He wasn't punishing me but teaching me to trust His timing, He was teaching me patience. He was teaching how to trust Him and how to accept the "no's" without falling apart. Changing my perspective helped me to see that failure wasn't my problem, pride was.

I conditioned myself to believe that hearing "no" was unacceptable and a sign of defeat. What stands true is that if I truly was going to be able to withstand success, hearing some "no's" was exactly what I needed to appreciate it when showed up. Failure must always be a friend because it proceeds success.

Failure is the antidote for the spirit of arrogance and pride. To be wrong, to mess up horribly to the point it can't be repaired invites the spirit of humility in. It's like sage to a new house. Walking in humility rids us of the thinking that it has to be our way, one way, and no other way. It exposes you to new ideas and invites you to a broader understanding of how to avoid the pitfalls of the past and this time, pass the test! Without humility, you will learn just how deceptive and misleading your own thoughts can truly be.

I have to constantly read the scripture that keeps a "sistah" in check. It tells me to lean not on my own understanding, in all my ways acknowledge Him, and He will direct my path. All that thinking I had overtaxed my brain with in my 20's and 30's. I could have enjoyed the quality of my life a whole lot more. Sistah, after all you've been through, you deserve to leave your past behind by asking God to make you over with a new identity in Him and be willing to change your perspective so that you can walk freely in that new identity.

What brings me the greatest peace today is knowing that the name my parents chose, was actually aligned with the divine order that God had set from the start. I know that no matter what name, title or tag I wear, I know my true God-given identity. I know that I wasn't an afterthought or a failure but His Child, His daughter and His Own. He stayed with me as I endured the identity crisis; only to fix the crisis by changing the way I viewed the crisis. He loved me enough to bring about a change in me because He knew my name from the very start.

People spend their whole lives searching for a sense of belonging. They search for it in people and things in hopes of establishing an identity to feel a part of something. But disappointment comes when we never quite find it. For me, I'm now proud to have a new name as a reminder that just like Abraham, Sarah, and Jacob, I was given a new identity for purpose. The meaning of my first name taught me that I must know who I am and stay alert, and my middle name reminds me to reach and strive for something greater than myself. Any progression I made would have to be grounded in the Creator.

"For I know the plans I have for you," says the LORD. "They are plans for good and not for disaster, to give you a future and a hope." Jeremiah 29:11

We live by so many titles and names, and that's who we are identified as, but who are you? Are you living your life by what the world has imposed on you, what you have told yourself, or what God has shown you?

In order to move forward in life, you must understand your identity and who God uniquely created you to be. As divine beings, we all were created to have unique identities, characteristics and purposes. Our identity can only be discovered when we truly come close to our Creator. It allows you to grow in a way that looks like the Creator himself. Let's be clear, that doesn't mean you will one day reach His perfection but it does mean that you can live with His presence. For me, that's perfection. His presence provides confidence. Not arrogance in myself but confidence in everything He said I could do or be. So many women lack their God-given confidence because they struggle with identity. We depend on misogynistic TV shows, our friends or men who have no idea who they are to tell us what and who we are and ought to be. We make what they say the gospel not recognizing the slow diminishing process of

having our self-worth and esteem disappear. What must be considered is that there is the Creator who has final authority on what you shall be.

The Bible tells us of the conversation that Jesus had with His disciples concerning identity. In Matthew 16,13-19, He asked them, *"Who do people say I am?"* The disciples responded to what others thought Jesus was. Then Jesus threw the question at them, *"Who do you say I am?"* Simon replied, *"You are the Christ, the son of the Living God."*

Regardless of what others thought of Him, He knew who He was with boldness and confidence. To move forward in life, we need to have that same confidence. Without it, we won't have the ability to persevere in the face of adversity. Remember our identity is important. It can only be found in who we are as it relates to our relationship with the one who created us, God. He is the only one that can kill the crisis.

From this day forward, don't allow yourself to forget that.

Chapter 3

The Dreamer in Me

As a child, I loved to sit and daydream about any and everything. I would look up to the sky and imagine myself living there with clouds shaped as people and they would be my new friends. I would daydream about what I would become when I grew up. I remember being so confident and telling anyone who'd listen about what my life would be like one day. By the time I hit middle school, my mind was made up. All I had to do was grow up. I remember sitting in that class waiting to take the national vocational test to determine what type of career field would best fit me. I never questioned my results because I knew exactly who I wanted to be. I just knew the test would agree with me. I was so excited to hear the results that would be read from the teacher in front of the class. I couldn't wait to have it confirmed that I would be a fashion designer or the chef that I had always hoped I would be. And not just any chef, I would be one of those chefs that had their own TV show or one of those fashion designers that traveled the world. Everyone would be wearing what I created. What a life that I had concocted in my head for myself! Cooking and designing things on paper were some of my favorite past times.

I was such a BIG dreamer! As I heard the teacher read my results, my emotions went from excitement to sheer devastation. It said that the best career choice for me would be a manager or crew chief at a fast food restaurant and I was devastated. I listened as she read so many of my friends who according to this test, could become nurses, teachers, engineers, firefighters, and secretaries. But me, a manager at a fast food restaurant? I saw the smirks on their faces and heard their laughter when mine was read. Even from the teacher.

What will I do with all my big hopes and dreams now? No one would care about me styling anyone or I couldn't possibly get on a T.V. show cooking now! According to the test results, these things were for smarter people. According to this test, I had the lessor paying and lessor respected jobs. By the sound of their laughter, they knew it too. So, I began to operate on the level in which was spoken over me. It was at that time of my life that I started to dim my own light. The dreamer in me turned into self-esteem issues as I lived from a level of other people's perception of me. Now, don't get me wrong, even though I had great parents who told me that I could be anything I wanted to be, I couldn't receive their affirmations. Looking back, I think it was that experience of public humiliation that made me dumb myself down for a few years and see myself as less than. I passed the 8th grade but I stopped taking school so serious and did just enough to pass.

After all, I didn't need much education to be a fast food manager or crew chief. I began to hang around people who didn't strive too hard for anything, nor did I apply myself to things that demanded much from me. For a while, I thought that this wasn't bad because no one would expect too much. On the other hand, I constantly wrestled as I asked myself, "What will you do with the dreams that keep screaming that you can become so much more?"

My mother was a student at this time, attending VSU when it was called Virginia State College. Whenever she took me to class with her, I saw these girls coming across the campus marching in a group. I asked her who they were because they looked important and some kind of serious! She said those girls were sorority girls. I recall her saying that you had to go to college and make good grades to be one of those. Immediately, I pushed the thought away quickly because a voice kept screaming to me that I wasn't one of the smart people anymore. I felt disqualified way before I was even old enough to apply for college. I had already set myself apart from anything meaningful and good. It wasn't until some years down the road that I would encounter a teacher by the named of Ms. Burnett. I thought she was just extremely hard on me, even mean. As I look back, she would push me to do things outside of my comfort zone, like speaking in front of the class or putting me in charge of something. She looked past all my eye rolling and mumbling under my breath at her. She never gave me a choice on whether I wanted to do something or not. After I would do whatever it was she wanted, she would stand in front of me with her hands on her hips, smelling like Elizabeth Taylor's White Diamond and say, "Now that wasn't so bad, was it? It was in you all along girl with ya hard-headed self!" Although I acted as though I didn't, I liked her because she didn't hesitate in returning the same eye roll I had given her. She would tell me that I could do and be anything that I wanted to be, and it was really up to me. I don't know when the shift came, but with her influence, I began to regain confidence within myself.

God will send people who will pour positivity in your life to rebuild you after you have been broken down. At some point, I stopped hearing the echo of my previous teacher's voice and classmates' laughter as the results of the test that was read and started listening to another voice that I later in life recognized as the voice of God. It was telling me that I could do all things. It was important for me to start trusting myself with myself. What the teacher spoke out loud about me made me feel that what I thought about myself was false and what the test said was the truth. I felt stupid for believing ME! What a trick the devil tried to play on me at such a young age.

I thank God that the devil didn't have more power than God and the fact that he wasn't able to make that little test be my testimony. God silenced the voices that said, "This is all you can do and being a restaurant manager is as far you will go in life". Here's where the importance of persevering past the disappointments in life is necessary. When you keep living, in spite of how you feel, what's been said about you or spoken over you, you will discover that there is more than can be developed in you, more potential in you, and more ability than people will ever give you credit for. This is where you must believe in you. You will be one of your biggest investments and the return is promising when you trust yourself.

The choice to believe in myself led me into the year 2010. I not only managed but also owned my own restaurant called 23:1 Bistro. The name derived from the 23rd Psalms (The Lord is my Shepherd, I shall not want). I employed over thirty people and a few of them were my classmates from that very same 8th grade class. And that oldest daughter of mine ended up graduating from Johnston and Wales as a chef. For me, this was my "Won't He do it?!" moment! I understood what God meant when He said that He was able to do much more than what we could ask or think through His power working in us. The thing about dreaming big is that it has no time frame, cap or limit. It can only be minimized if you allow it to. Never allow people to speak something over your life that contradicts the gifts and talents that are in you and what God says about you because truly God has the final say. People will come and go but your dreams are yours forever! I have learned that dreaming big comes with big requirements. You have to push past pessimistic people and people who won't encourage your goals and dreams. You know the type. The "I wouldn't do that if I were you" folk or the folks that say "Oh" or " "Must be nice" when you tell them the great things that's happening in your life. You will discover that the "Oh" folks are the same as the "No" folks that mean you NO good.

People who are truly supportive of you will always in some way be a blessing to what you dream about. They will show up and push you, encourage you, and speak to your fear and insist that it will not hinder you. They are there to help support your purpose not steer you from it. They will build you up and not tear you down. They want you to win.

Those people are the opposite of the pessimistics. They are the "Purpose Pushers". Everyone needs a "Purpose Pusher" in their lives. Living without purpose pushers is like having a brand new car, no gas, and with absolutely nowhere to go. Chances are, you won't get very far. With support, you'll go further than what you couldn't have imagined! Go back and reclaim that dream you set aside. You may be just like me. You may have listened to the wrong voices and they made those dreams appear unattainable. The truth is, they're still waiting for you. Everything you need is already on the inside of you. Keep dreaming.

Dreams will lead you to a Purpose that unlocks the doors to Perseverance!

Your greatest weapon to purpose is to dream again and do the things that set your soul on fire or at least create a spark. No matter what it takes, hold on tight to your dreams. It doesn't matter how long it takes for you to see it happen. If the dream was placed in your heart and mind, then there is something you're supposed to accomplish with it. Don't ignore it forever. Ask the Creator for insight, get quiet, and prepare to receive what is revealed to you. The word tells us that faith without works is dead. Therefore, you have a part that only you can do. Set goals that will inspire you on the journey and then take action to make your dreams come to fruition.

What skills and strengths do you have that can take you to your next level? I'm convinced that God has given us skills and abilities that will launch us into our next level of life's achievements but having these skills are not enough. We have to make a conscious effort to step out of our comfort zone and do what makes us most fearful. I've discovered that fear is just an opportunity to operate in faith.

Faith will require that you make a decision. It forces you to trust God. It pushes you to trust and believe in yourself no matter how the odds seemed stacked up against you. It encourages you to let go of what was said and done and to move in the direction of what you've dreamed about.

Soon you'll move from dreaming to living in the divine purpose you were called to. Taking a Spiritual Gifts Assessment test can equip you with knowledge and a greater understanding of who you are in God. This will allow you to see how you can begin or continue to move forward with purpose and power. Prayerfully, you will see that dreams really do come true!

Chapter 4

A Grateful Soul

After years of owning and operating a group home for boys, I realized that even though I had a mom, aunties, sisters and daughters of my own, I was around my male counterparts more. I was missing the connection that I naturally had with women. I had begun to think about the connections I was missing all the time. I recalled how I would have some of the best conversations with the women in my family. I always enjoyed their company when we would get together and a few close friends. Anyone else were random interactions which entailed some quick encounter in the mall, at the grocery store, a few minutes here or there at church or just these random lunch dates with an old friend. There was nothing concrete. There was nothing that would provide or give me the connection I was seeking.

I longed for this more than I had realized. I wanted to have connections that were long lasting, meaningful, and spiritual. I was out shopping for shoes and if anyone knows me, this is truly one of my favorite past times. While shopping, it hit me! A shoe store! That's it! I'd open up a shoe store for women. Just like that, I said I was going to call it "A Diva Shoe!" Boom! Just like that. Now, of course, this would

place women together who were fly all the time and loved
high heels like me.

I went home and started writing down some ideas. I
surfed the Internet on everything about shoes. I went ahead
and told everybody about my new adventure! But for some
reason, I could not get the information that I needed to really
get started. I asked friends and called other stores to see
where they had gotten their shoes from and still nothing! It
all seemed like I kept hitting brick walls but never finding the
inner works to the shoe business. I was getting frustrated
already. There had to be some answers. After all, other people
did it, right?

A few days later, a tragic incident occurred at my group
home for boys. The incident had resulted in the death of one
of my clients. I was devastated and numb at the same time.
We had never experienced anything like this and didn't
know how we would tell the parents of this child that died in
our place of business. How do I comfort other clients that
had witnessed this? My business swarmed in with detectives,
state investigators, and the media. They all camped outside to
get the details of what had happened. I didn't know what to
do or where to go for peace. Everyone who wanted
immediate answers were calling my name, and because I
wasn't present when the incident happened, I didn't have any
statements to make. In the midst of the confusion, I could
remember stepping outside on the porch of the group home,

away from everyone, and I began to pray. It was not a long prayer, but I remember looking out at all the police cars, TV station trucks, and the state investigators' cars lined up and down the street.

Feeling so overwhelmed at that moment, I remember saying, *"God, please be with us."* I stood there a few minutes more and began to feel peaceful. I also felt like I could see what was happening all around me, but something was very calm over me, and my mind felt clear.

I had no choice but to put my attention solely to this situation. Shoes seemed so trivial in comparison to someone's life being lost. My business came under investigation. We were later found not guilty of any wrongdoing, still in compliance with the state and cleared to resume business. My mind always goes back to that moment on the porch, where it was just me and God. Such a short prayer gave me everything I needed to survive. Peace.

I learned that in the midst of a crisis, you must step away from it all and just ask God to be with you. No long drawn out speeches to God about what He already knows and no affirming the confusion around you. Just simply God, be with me. I realized that in the most overwhelming times of your life, being alone with God will bring the peace, strength, and clarity that you will need to face the fight, whatever your fight may be. I left the porch and entered back into my fight knowing that I wasn't in the fight alone. God was with me.

Months had passed and business seemed to be getting back into a flow. Because of the incident at my business, prayers just became a part of my daily routine. Because I began to see the power in praying, I wanted God to continue to stay with me. Through this new prayer life, for the first time, I began to see God as a friend.

The thought of opening up the shoe store returned. But this time, I started to pray and asked God if that was what he wanted for me. I began telling God about my desire to connect with other women. I reminded God about always wanting to be a designer. Subsequently, I continued to thank God for how He saw us through that ordeal and grateful that He didn't leave me. I remember sitting there praying and all of a sudden, I started crying. It wasn't your typical cry. I began to ball! It wasn't sadness I was feeling. I was overtaken with gratefulness.

The more I cried, I began screaming, "Thank you, God! Thank you, God!" I know that the time of praise was only a few minutes but it felt like hours. The truth of this is that I don't think I had ever praised God like that before. I had watched others in church run, jump, shout, and cry like a baby. I even rolled my eyes when I felt they were doing too much or carried on for too long. This time, it was me and I couldn't even stop it. There was something on the inside of me that was in complete control.

I remember sitting there trying to collect myself and to remember what I was doing before this happened. I was praying about the shoe store! I began to think about how grateful I was to have this new prayer life with God that was birthed out of such a painful place. I was thankful that we had made it through in spite of the loss of life. I kept saying the word grateful over and over again and it just stuck. I thought about the shoes, and there it was! The name of the shoe store: "Grateful Soles".

I started smiling so hard and jumping up and down because the name was so perfect. I knew God gave that to me and I knew I was on to something! I kept saying the name out loud, and the more I said it, the more I began to see it in my mind. I logged onto my computer and wrote it out just to see how it would look like when written down and wow! "Grateful Soles Shoe Boutique" was it.

The longer I stared at the name, I knew that this was going to be more than a new business venture. I saw it as God introducing me to my new purpose. One of the lessons I learned during this ordeal with the group home incident was that God allowed that trial to enter into my life to bring me to a place of humility. You see, when I originally wanted to open up a shoe store, I didn't ask God for His help. I didn't ask Him to be with me. I didn't even ask Him if this was what He even wanted me to do. I just started doing what I wanted to do.

I started sharing my plans with everyone and became frustrated when I couldn't get any information on how to get started. I had totally left God out. I understand now that if I was to do anything from this point on, I needed God to be with me. What happened to the original name of the shoe store "A Diva Shoe Boutique" you ask? I learned that God had to bring that trial in my life to transform how I viewed myself into what He wanted me to be. You see, for this new purpose in my life, God didn't need me to be a DIVA. He needed me to be GRATEFUL, a Grateful Soul.

I didn't rush to share the good news with everyone like I had done before, but God placed a woman of God in my spirit who I had always admired. She was a businesswoman in retail with incredible style and integrity. I reached out to her and she didn't hesitate to pour information into me. She sent me to people who owned shoe businesses that didn't mind sharing with me on how they got started. From there, I was able to attend my first shoe vendor's show in Atlanta. That was a dream come true. She talked to me about integrity and how to conduct myself as a woman in business. She once told me that, "All a woman has in this world is her good name." Those words of wisdom will stay with me forever. Thank you Dianna, I will always love and appreciate you for that.

It seemed like God just started opening doors that were previously shut. I started hosting home shoe parties regularly to the point I needed a storefront. I prayed about it and I knew that God was still with me. I took a walk down Old town Petersburg and walked into a shop. The lady told me that she was going to be moving out and she put me in contact with the owners. Within days, I had the keys to my new boutique. The owners loved the name so much that they were willing to build.

I didn't know the impact that this little boutique in Old Town Petersburg would make. I didn't know God had it for me to be the first African American woman to own and operate a shoe boutique in the City of Petersburg. I didn't know that I would be used to distribute shoes to the homeless miles away from me and as far as to third world countries. I didn't know that God would allow me to host sold-out Fashion Shoe Shows and be able to vend my products from state to state. The places I would go and people I would meet for the next five years was mind-blowing!

I learned the lesson that when you go to God, you can really see the power of Him moving on the inside of you in ways your mind couldn't have even dreamed of, not even on your best day. You will understand what His will and not your will or way truly means. God has a way of thinking that is so different from the scope of how our human capacity can think. He sees what's ahead of us. So it's important to follow His leading and not attempt to lead ourselves. Without him, we really don't know where we are headed or where we will end up. That, my sisters, is a scary place to be in!

"God, be with me" can ignite a new and lasting relationship between you and Him that will bring you to a place of gratefulness and will open doors to your purpose.

It's about Perspective

You will encounter so many events in life. The not so pleasant ones can often change your perspective on the way you view life if you can pray and ask God for the strength to see things differently. If you are analyzing your situation from a place of defeat, you will feel defeated, you will feel there is no way out, and the only option is to give up.

Disappointments can make a person cynical and bitter. After a while, you won't even recognize you have left a place of peace and stepped over the threshold of negative emotions and actions.

Does any of this sound familiar?

- Prepare for the worst for all situations.

- Discourage others when giving advice instead of supporting them.

- Fault Finders: judgmental of others while doing the same behaviors.

- Suspicious about everyone's motive when approached with kindness.

- Can't seem to enjoy celebratory times.

- Allowing fear to preoccupy your thoughts to the point you become anxious about it.

- Believing that your past has more significance and value, so you allow it to dictate your emotions and behavior today.

A cynical person is someone whose thoughts will always be negative. They think their own selfishness motivates everyone. They often see the world as cold and harsh. In order to survive in it, they feel that they must give back to the world the same cold and harsh dispositions they receive. The reality is that underneath all the negativity is just a very hurt and disappointed person who just needs to be healed.

That's why perspective is so important. The wonderful part is that it can be changed.

When you're able to see things from a more positive outlook, you and everything around you will begin to shift for the better. Two people could be faced with the same set of circumstances but the one who saw the problem as an opportunity to challenge their growth will be the one who unlocks the doors to new possibilities and awareness of gratitude even in the toughest of times. If you are striving towards a better perspective, try these for yourself:

- Pray and ask God to give you a new way of seeing your life, ask Him to transform your thinking.

- Don't allow negative thoughts to take up residence. Throw those thoughts out like trash!

- Be open to welcoming new ideas and suggestions.

- Stay away from gossip. Don't listen and don't do it!

- Watch your speech. Speak with optimism. "I got this!" Declare what you'd like to see. "That promotion is mine!" When things don't go the way you've hoped say, "there is something better waiting for me."

- Be mindful of your body language and outward appearance. Smile in the face of your challenges. Keep your head up and back straight. Keep your hair together. Change your earrings daily. Throw on a print you've dared to wear. Remember, it's about "Perspective"!

- Take ownership of where you are. You can't fix what you don't face.

- Count the good and bad in your life as all blessings.

- Pray daily!

Apostle Paul was one man who learned the art of being grateful in the midst of great adversity. While writing in Ephesians 5:20, shortly before his imprisonment in Rome, he stated that we should give thanks always for all things unto God and the father in the name of our Lord Jesus Christ.

What would make a man who is facing time be grateful in that season of his life, especially when it seemed so grim? Just like Paul, He found the good in his bad situation.

There is so much that we can be grateful for, but it's about that perspective piece. If the other steps aren't where you are, there is a place where we can all start at. We often forget to start with just being happy. We are alive. Notice I didn't say, alive and well. It takes time to get to being well. Start with being grateful for life. That alone is a great place to begin living a life of gratefulness. After that, just add the fact that you didn't buy the air you breathe or the people in your life. Just keep adding and it will become evident that you have far more positive going on than what you think.

Gratitude is a healing aid. Practicing gratitude daily helps you to heal from the inside out and move forward in your life.

In fact, gratitude may be one of the most overlooked tools that we all have access to every day. Cultivating gratitude doesn't cost a thing, and it certainly doesn't take much time but the benefits are enormous. Do you want to build a strong foundation for your house? Have an attitude of gratitude.

Gratitude opens the door to healthier relationships

Showing appreciation can help you win new friends, according to a 2014 study published in *Emotion.* The study found that thanking a new acquaintance makes them more likely to seek an ongoing relationship. So whether you thank a stranger for doing something kind for you or you send a quick thank-you note to that co-worker who helped you with a project, acknowledging other people's contributions can lead to new opportunities.

Gratitude promotes better physical health

People who express daily acts of gratitude experience fewer aches and pains and they report feeling healthier than other people, according to a 2012 study published in *Personality and Individual Differences.* Grateful people are also more likely to take care of their health. They exercise more often and are more likely to attend regular check-ups with their doctors. This is likely to contribute to further longevity. The fitness centers are packed with grateful people who have suffered strokes, heart attacks, and more. If you ask any of them why they were there, I'm sure they would say how grateful they were to have a second chance at life and good health. I'm sure many would respond with gratefulness for being able to have the activity of their limbs, to just be out around others and not in a hospital bed. They have developed an understanding of gratefulness and most times, it's through their trials that they were now able to adopt that newfound mentality.

Count life lessons as you count your blessings

A wise man once said, "Experience is the best teacher of all things and only God can make all things work together for good." We often get upset when we experience tough times in life and want them to disappear quickly. However, it's in the midst of a crucial time, a time when everything seems to be falling apart around you, just when it seems things were just coming together, when the unthinkable, the unimaginable happens and the irreversible tragedies shows up, the thing that comes and shakes up our very foundation that makes you want to question your very existence. That place is most often referred to as the wilderness. If we don't give up there, on the other side of all the trauma is where you'll be able to look back and really see the power in us working, the strength, the peace to survive and the power to keep going. The more you share with others all that you have endured, not from a place of victimization but a place of victory, it will produce healing for them and more gratitude for you. This positions you as an agent of change in the lives of everyone you encounter. The beauty of God and His wisdom is that He had it for me to endure so that I could share this message of gratitude with you. A beautiful shoe store named Grateful Soles may have been where it all began but it was always in God's plan that Grateful Souls is where we should all end. *1Thessalonians 5:16-18_ "Rejoice always, pray continually, give thanks in all circumstances; for this is God's will for you in Christ Jesus".*

Chapter 5

What's in Your House?

"So Elisha said to her... what do you have in your house...?"

~ 2Kings 4:2

After twenty years of building a marriage, building a family, building businesses, and building my faith in God, I still found myself among the many who have had to endure the pain and destruction of divorce. It felt like all those years of building what I thought was a good life all came crumbling down. A wife, mother, and businesswoman was replaced with my new role as a single mom, no job, and home foreclosed on all in the same year. Honestly, I wasn't ready mentally, physically or emotionally. I was not ready, and neither were my children. The hurt and disappointment were visible on my children's very skin. I functioned numbly in my new existence while covering it with a smile. The appearance of strength was my minute-by-minute goal. Even if that meant I would have sacrifices and avoid what was truly going on in the inside. All in all, I continued practicing gratitude for what I still had, while grieving over all that I had to let go of. After all those years and all those roles of being everything to everyone, I would now have to rediscover who I was as a woman.

In 2012, God had called me to ministry. As I was attempting to grow and develop in the word of God, I remember when I first shared with my Bishop that I believed God was calling me to preach or something. I can still see his face when he looked over at me and said, "Now? With all you got going on? I remember him telling me that everything in my life was about to change. I was thinking to myself, "of course, it will change". More of God. Who doesn't want that? But my understanding of what God was going to do and who He had to remove to prepare me for this journey with Him was way more than what I had ever imagined. I would need God like never before for all the things that started happening around me, almost instantly. Shortly after this talk with my Bishop about my new journey in ministry, I got the news that my only brother was dying of cancer. Six months later, he was gone at age 40. It seemed like attending funerals had become a part of my monthly schedule. One loss after another had consumed me and my family for one whole year. I didn't realize that this was the beginning of a shift. I had accepted a role in leadership, serving as the Chairperson over my church's women's ministry. But here I was, trying to lead in ministry and deal with my own issues, at the same time, behind the scenes. I had heard the term "leading while bleeding". It was now my new reality and I felt and tasted the blood first hand. With all the deaths of loved ones, my household was floating between the five stages of grief daily. Nothing could have prepared me but God for what I was about to face: the unexpected end of my sixteen-year marriage. I strived to appear strong on the outside because that's what I thought was expected of me. I kept going. I tried to keep the hurt to myself until I could get to a place where I could take care of my daughters and myself independently. They became my reasons to forge ahead. I needed something to motivate me and they became it. Even though keeping the hurt to myself wouldn't have been the advice or the counseling I would have given another woman going through the same thing, the shock and numbness wouldn't allow me to feel past anything deeper than what I need to do for us to survive financially. I kicked into survival mode. I had ignored the overwhelming feelings of sadness, spontaneous tears that I refused to let fall or let anyone see. The nervousness and chest pains were covered with cute blouses and the wall I had built up around my heart. My trust in people was diminishing. I was vulnerable and I protected myself the best I knew how at the time. I would stop the hemorrhaging by putting up some new and stronger walls. This time they were made of brick. My house was brick wall strong and I told myself that no one was ever getting in again. I know I'm not alone.

I had taken on the strong black woman syndrome. My mindset at the time was, "I'm going to get through this thing, with bells on and I'm not going to miss a beat!" Looking back, I realized that type of thinking actually did more harm than good to me and I am sure to those I was called to serve too. The most intimate part of my life was being played out like a Lifetime movie without my permission. I felt like I no longer had the rights to my life story. I didn't even recognize the characters that were playing myself. I knew there were cracks in the walls but we had overcome so many in 16 years, surely we'd survive anything else. I was always confident that the foundation was still strong. But my house was crumbling while I was still taking up residence. My pipes were bursting with abuse. Toilets were leaking. Flies and termites had boldly made their way in every corner of each room. Even though I saw what was happening, I was already addicted to familiarity and a worshipper of the memories As beautiful as my home looked on the outside with an immaculate manicured lawn, perfectly cut shrubs and beautifully bloomed flowers that gave the appearance of life, the inside of my house was inhabitable to live in. Whether I'd liked it or not, it was time to go.

My house was crumbling around me. Money had run out and nothing was coming in. I was in school full time and searching for a job. I looked for anything to make ends meet. I tried to keep a public face that everything was fine and that my life wasn't falling apart. However, the reality of my situation had hit home. I would go to church dressed up every Sunday and by that afternoon showering at the local YMCA because our water had been shut off. There were many days the girls and I would eat at the dining hall at my school so we would have a meal for that night. I had never felt more connected to God but still very lost in my life all at the very same time. The feeling of failure came back with a vengeance.

I remember a January day with the weather being very crisp while waiting for my daughter to come down the stairs to take her to her practice. I was struggling with the reality that I no longer had my business to support me. I had two children to raise that stared back at me with confused faces and sad eyes. They looked to me for all the answers to make things better as I still had unanswered questions of my own.

How did my life get here when I thought I was doing everything right? I was a family woman. I served in the church. I didn't run the streets. I loved my family but yet I was here? How would I pay for all these mounting bills that were now on me? What would my next move be now that my life had changed suddenly? How would I protect my children from what they heard and saw when I knew they were not ready to face it? So many questions and not enough answers. Just a lot of change. As I sat there waiting, I recalled the time my Bishop had said, "Everything in your life is going to change." I ask myself and God, "Is this what he meant?" It couldn't be!

I watched my daughter as she walked down the steps and opened an empty refrigerator. After handing her a pop-tart, we left on a near-empty tank of gas to take her to her practice. I thought it was better for her to be there than to stay at home and absorb the stench of sadness and depression that loom over our heads day by day. I did not only busy myself, I made their life busy too. After dropping her off, I drove back and began to cry out to God, "Lord, I'm in trouble, and I don't know why or how I got here. I don't know how I'm going to do this, I don't know how I'm going to take care of my daughters". Through tear-filled eyes, I began to give God a list of the things I didn't have and on top of that, I had to prepare a sermonic presentation. Lord, this is too much! Somehow over my crying, over the song playing on the radio station, I heard a calm voice say, "What's in your house?" It dawned on me that I had remembered seeing something in the Bible about a widowed woman. So I asked, God, "What does that have to do with me and what I got going on?!" I kept hearing, "It's in your house". So, when I got back to my home, I pulled out my phone and did what most people did. I googled the story for the first time. I immediately could identify with the widow. She had two children, her husband was gone, and she was just desperately trying to make ends meet. She tried so hard to find a way to pay her debt so that her children wouldn't be sold into slavery and could survive. That was me! I read about how Prophet Elisha had asked her about what she may have had in her house and how she replied by telling him about the jars she had. Only an hour prior, my mind was overwhelmed with worry. It was now intriguingly consumed with the life of this woman. I began to write and write. Before I knew it, God had given me my sermonic presentation. The more I wrote, I started to see that God was not just giving me her story but giving me instructions for my life too. It stood out so clear in the text about how she didn't think the flask of oil was worth anything. How often do we do that as women? Minimize the quality of what we have inside of us? Hmmm...

So, I started looking around in my house because "It's in your house" continued to ring in my ear. I looked in the closet and didn't see anything but when I went into my garage, I started to see so many things that looked valuable. Some of those things had been packed up for years in there. I had passed them many times and never looked over at them. Today, I could see things so clearly. It appeared to be wall to wall of things that my ex-husband had left behind. I left the garage and sat back down to continue reading the story. I had gotten to the part where Prophet Elisha had given her instructions. He told her to borrow as many empty jars as she could from her friends and neighbors. Next, she was to go into her house with her sons, shut the door behind her and pour the olive oil from her flask into the jars. It went on to say how she set each one aside until they were filled. Now, her sons kept bringing her jars, and she kept filling them until every container was full to the brim! Long story short, the woman had gone back to Prophet Elisha and told him what she had done, and it said that he directed her to sell the olive oil and pay her debts. He told her that if she did that, then she and her sons could live on what was left over. I jumped up from that table and went back to the garage. I felt a surge of energy that I hadn't had in weeks. I felt I was being guided. I looked around that garage and started seeing the value in everything that I had. Things that I had purchased and forgot about years ago began to appear, still brand new in bags! I grabbed my keys and backed my Envoy up to the door of the garage. I started loading up everything that I saw of value. I had so much stuff. Just like the widow, I kept filling that truck to the brim! When I couldn't get any more in, I headed to the local pawnshop and sold what I had. I left there with enough to pay my bills, buy groceries, fill up my tank and invest in some jewelry to start my jewelry business. My children and I were able to live off of what was left. I must say that God has truly been good to me.

He allowed my oil to keep flowing because I still sell jewelry today. I gave that sermonic presentation with God's power and conviction because He had me to live it first. God showed me that everything I needed to go on living was in me all along. Even though I had some things on the inside of my house that was causing destruction, He showed me that if I just followed His instructions, He would fix everything that was broken. He reminded me that I didn't have to look far and hard. The oil He gave to the widow was the same oil that is also in you and me. A lot of times, the solution is less complicated than what we make it to be. It is a matter of trusting what we don't understand, comprehend or when we don't foresee a positive end. As I planned the women's ministry's first conference, God had me to name it, "The Fresh Oil Conference." I knew someone else needed to be reminded about the power of God that's in us all if we allow it to be activated. The peace, comfort, healing, forgiveness, and the strength that I needed to move forward with my life all came when the power of God entered into my house.

God had called me to serve women. It's funny how I thought that He had prepared me for ministry because of all of the experience that I had working with women in business and because I had been married for 16 years, great kids, and the look of success, right? You would think that should have qualified me to lead other women, right? But what I know about God now is that He is not interested in the house you or I chose to build for us. When He wants to use us, He wants us to be under His reconstruction, even if this means that He has to evict some longtime residence and bulldozer that whole thing down to start completely over. At the end of the day,

God intends on having His way for His purpose and His plan whether you like it or not. God is strategic, brilliant, and the God of second chances.

The Almighty did not require me to pretend to have it all together, especially when the women that I was called to serve needed transparency. They were women who needed to relate to hurt, disappointment, and how to overcome by the power of God. They needed a knocked down, dragged-through-the-mud type of leader that got back up and smacked that mud off their faces. They needed someone who showed them how to still trust in God, despite it all. They needed to witness in front of them a representation of God's grace and what it looks like to be redeemed of time. I didn't truly feel qualified until my walls were stripped, the rug was pulled back, and all you could see was the dust. I'm thankful for the dust because this experience introduced me to so many women and men who needed encouragement from a living testimony. The Bible says that it was good that I was afflicted. I can say that now. It was in this season, God tore down that house, He changed and rearranged my living conditions, and for the first time in a long time, I began to embrace and enjoy my space, free of clutter and things that were no longer useful. When God removes things from you, it at first can be devastating emotionally. Once the emotions settle, there are usually instructions that follow for your next move. Quiet your spirit. Listen and begin to write down everything you hear from God. He is preparing you for your next place. Just because it's been there a long time doesn't mean it can go. What we've allowed in our house to take up residence simply cannot relocate with us. We have to remember, it's not about where we are, it's about where God is trying to take us. Just know that for a season, you may have to go it alone, and that's okay too. That alone season can be used to restore your mind, body, and spirit, to get to know you again. God gave me a new foundation to stand on, not money, not a business, and not a man. He gave me Him. He gave me something stable, long-lasting, and committed to withstand any storm that will come in my life. This time around, my house is built by the power of God.

I'm reminded of an old hymn I used to hear my Granma Savannah sing...

My Hope Is Built On Nothing Less

Edward Mote   John Bacchus Dykes

Now, what did you say that was in your House?

"Anyone who listens to my teaching and follows it is wise, like a person who builds a house on solid rock." ~ Mathew 7:24

Chapter 6

You Hold The Keys!

The Power of Discernment

It would be easy to continue discussing the power of God, how that power divinely is in us and how God can use that same power to work through us, but as women, we often struggle to address the power in us. We just give it away. In order to truly move to a place of power, we must identify the part in which we played to hinder our own progression. We not only struggle to address it but some of us just flat out refuse to even admit or take ownership, not even to ourselves.

"To know the truth and the truth shall set you free", what a profound statement that is.

I have encountered some of the bravest and most intelligent women who have looked trials and obstacles in the face and smiled. Things I simply couldn't fathom experiencing and somehow they found the strength to keep going. But I have also observed some of those same heroic women while trying to be this word we love to use so freely: "strong" so that they could also keep going, not realizing that they were still vulnerable and unhealed. Strong women struggle with this word because we often times equate it with being weak. The reality is that in times of experiencing life-changing events, we are vulnerable and it's okay. The problem is that nobody told us that it was okay. Being vulnerable during a crisis is like having an open scab or lying in your house in your bed with the front door wide open or laying your big key ring down. I mean the one that holds your car, house and work keys, and you don't have a clue as to where they may be! Now your guard is down and the things you hold ownership to have now become susceptible to anything that wants to enter in. This is bound to happen when we fail to protect one of the most sacred and delicate things that we own, our heart.

I had to grow up a lot in God and go through many things before I was truly able to understand this one. This scripture is not for the faint of heart. You have to have gone through giving what's important to you away and learning the lessons that came with it to get this one.

Proverbs 4:23-27, *"Above all else, guard your heart, for everything you do flows from it."*

The challenge of being a good person is that good people genuinely have kind hearts and want to see the best in everyone and everything. You are not a person who runs to do harm to others. In fact, you are accepting of the underdogs. You help the hurting and want to nurture the wounded. The challenge of this natural way of being is that often times you can become vulnerable to the opposite, which is evil. A kind-hearted spirit with good intentions can become prey to things that may appear to give peace, comfort, or an escape from the trauma that comes with unexpected life-changing events.

I don't think there is a woman alive, well and in her right mind that would just invite trauma into her life if she hadn't been in a place of vulnerability first. Often in the African American culture, but not limited to this culture, black women presume that the more you are able to endure and still be able to breathe afterwards, you are considered to be a strong woman to be admired and viewed as an overcomer. We sometimes have this notion that we are to wear that pain as a badge of honor and as our symbol of making it through what was designed to kill us. We come together over women conferences titled, "I'm An Overcomer" and "I Am A Survivor,". Destiny's Child had many women pumping it in their cars, ringtones, t-shirts and their favorite workout song at the gym. We swapped testimonies while reliving step by step the events, nursing and rehearsing every dirty deed that was done play by play and praising God that we were in a different place now. We received hugs and encouragement from our fellow Sistahs who had similar stories in the malls, restaurants, and beauty salons, you name it. Being superwoman is a powerful display of iron sharpening iron and having strength in numbers. Unfortunately, it has no real power of a testimony that is designed to heal others if we avoid dealing with the actual healing process and only focus on the play by play of the events. Too many of us get stuck on the level events and never elevate to experience true healing.

To truly overcome traumatic events, you must;

- Look at all perspectives, even the side that doesn't belong to you.

- Talk about the event and ensure that it doesn't cause destruction to your emotional well-being.

- Practice forgiveness (Forgiveness is not out of sight out of mind either. It's also a process that doesn't always happen overnight).

- Self evaluate and ask yourself about the part that you may have played and own it. It's rarely its ALL some else's fault.

- When you can pray for them and mean it, you're beginning to elevate.

- If you are not here yet, keep testifying how God is healing you. Keep declaring your strength but keep working on YOU so you no longer have to pretend to be healed. You'll know, feel, see and embrace it.

When we avoid the process of healing, we are rejecting the power of the Holy Spirit to deliver us from the company of seducing spirits that often disguises themselves as pain relief. These are all traps of the enemy who comes to kill, steal and destroy. If you let it and if you stay in a silent pain in order to keep the peace, you'll eventually start a war within yourself. What you're doing is telling the one who can help you to leave your house and inviting the spirit of anxiety, depression, sexual immorality, drinking, smoking, overspending, overeating and more in to take over your space. These demonic houseguests don't just go when asked to. They must be derived out. God asks of us to guard our hearts because they are precious. He knows that out of it comes the things that are most important: your wisdom and your peace. Those are your keys that you will need to protect your house. When you leave those keys down anywhere, you are leaving your heart open and vulnerable to hurt, disappointment, and sin. More often than not, we are guarding our hearts against our own demons and downfalls. The hurt comes from the sin and shame that we harbor inside and not always from those around us. Just remember, if you refuse to deal with it and heal, it will eventually deal with you. Now that doesn't give a person permission to become hard-hearted. The Bible says, "harden not our hearts" in the book of Hebrews. Therefore, we don't have permission to just create a brick wall up around our hearts so nothing or one can ever get in and nothing is ever flowing out.

I'll admit, it can be so easy to harden our hearts. It is easy to treat people the way they have treated us until we train ourselves to numb the feelings of vulnerability or weakness. If we do that, over time, we will become the hurt in someone else's life that we ourselves are trying to heal from. Hurt people always hurt people.

Another way good-hearted women give away their keys to the property they own is by disguising pain with busyness. I was trapped in what became a never-ending pace of busyness, multi-tasking, making ends meet, and constantly putting out fires, only to create more fires to put out another. Projects consumed my time before I had completed the previous. I found myself behaving similarly to many of the women in my life I knew that went through tough times. They would say, "I just stayed busy." When my mother had things on her mind, I recall her standing for hours, sweeping the floor, flowing from the den to the kitchen, cooking something or just moving around until she reached a solution. I mimicked what I saw and became an expert at being busy. The devil used this to distract me from healing properly. Because I stayed so busy, I didn't deal with anything deep within that would work against the numbness that I had gotten used to. I just adapted to the thought of "just keep going." The dangerous part of busyness, just like too much caffeine intake, is that you will eventually crash. That's why it is so important to be conscious on how you occupy your time when you're trying to move forward. Creating space and time to just be still is vital.

Give it Back

When I was pursuing my undergraduate degree majoring in Sociology at Virginia State University, I sat in a marriage & family class and my professor said something very profound. I left there with it forever etched in my brain. She said that we should stop holding on to other people's baggage. We should box it up and give it right back to them. In actuality, that's not what we do at all. We hold on to it long after they are gone. We become the caretaker of the belongings they left us with, and we store it for them instead of boxing their baggage up and giving it back. We protect toxic behavior with silence instead of throwing it away. I'm sure if you look down at your key ring, you have keys to things you don't even know what they are used for. But we keep them hoping we will find their usage again. What happens is that they end up using you. Using your time, resources, and peace of mind. Those things become heavy to carry and take up more storage in your house when you could have built an in-home gym. In order to move forward, you have to make up in your mind that the stuff must go but you're going to keep your keys. Stand up for yourself and give back what never really belonged to you. Choose to keep only what unlocks the door to new opportunities and renewed strength.

God kept reminding me in His word that He knew me a whole lot longer than I knew Him. He had plans specifically for me. The more I grew to know Him, the more that I would find that His love for me was deep. It was patient and real in the purest form. It was unconditional. I had strived but not arrived. I had spent a lot of time being carefree and careless to the thought of how deep God's love was for me. Instead I was busy. I mean really busy entertaining and loving any and everything that didn't have the capacity of loving me back. I've had to learn some hard lessons about not allowing busyness to distract me to the point I embraced the wrong people and things. I thought they would give me back what I gave to them, which in most cases, was all of me. Busyness can keep you distracted. None of the projects or the people can bring a true sense of wholeness. Only God alone can do that.

Anxiety is a best friend to busyness. Because we live in a society where we want immediate gratification, even from God, we're guilty of getting anxious when we can't always hear Him. Instead of waiting, while continuing to trust Him to cover those vulnerable places and to keep guard over our hearts, we lay our keys down for just anyone to pick up. I am sure someone who is reading this book has experienced or knows someone who has laid their keys down to one-sided relationships with friends, children, their spouses, coworkers or whoever. You know those relationships where someone loves or admires the other more. Relationships where someone gives more, and someone is more patient while the other person continually tests them. Someone may be kinder while the other person takes it for weakness. Someone gives more effort while the others person does the very least.

It can be exhausting to keep deeply loving someone or something from the purest part of your heart only to receive their rejection, inconsistencies, promises of doing better but with no real sign of their actions supporting their words. We can often relate to ourselves being treated this way in relationships, but when I began to write this chapter of the book, God reminded me that we often lay our keys down way before other people get involved. We've laid those keys down when we chose to live a life void of Him. He reminded me that He has been there waiting patiently after being repeatedly placed in the corner. He has always given without receiving. He has always been more patient than anyone else and yet, instead of inviting Him to live in the house He built, we prefer to give those keys to a stranger. However, we don't like it when people treat us the same. That hit home in a real way. Our relationship with the Creator must be first. It is the foundation. It helps us to be more selective in what keys, who, and what are the most important. The light bulb went off. God is the key! He unlocks every door. He gives access to blessings and favor. Because He is the Key, He is your power. He will protect you from hurt, harm, and danger. Those that are seen and unseen. God is the key that we can no longer afford to just lay down anywhere or let just anyone or anything have access.

There is something significantly important that we need along with guarding our hearts. We must have spiritual discernment. Discernment can be defined as being able to comprehend what is obscure, and a power to see what is not evident to the average mind. Spiritual discernment is the ability to tell the difference between truth and error. It is wisdom at its best, but it can only come from God. First, we must ask God for this gift and then as we face situations, we must ask God to continue to sharpen us. We must know the authentic so well that when the false appears, we can recognize it. By knowing and obeying the Word of God, we will train our ears and eyes with constant practice to distinguish good from evil on sight. We will know God's character and those who have God's character; we will know if that character displayed before us is something different.

The heart of spiritual discernment is being able to distinguish the voice of the world from the voice of God, to have a sense that "this is right" or "this is wrong." Spiritual discernment fends off temptation and allows us to "hate what is evil; cling to what is good" (Romans 12:9).

God gave us the house and keys but be careful who you allow to come in. Those keys belong to you! In moments of disparity, I have seen and had been a woman that gave what God said was rightfully mine over to seducing spirits that appeared as pain relief. I may have needed relief, but I needed discernment more. Without it, you're guaranteed to head toward more pain and problems than what you initially had.

Things will begin to crowd your space and after some time, you will have to ask that thing in which you've allowed to take over your house to let you in! I recall the famous movie by the late John Singleton, Baby Boy. Jodi was once again late picking Yvette up with her own car. After they experienced a break-up, she had become so used to him having her car and keys. She went out to the parking lot to look for him. Then, she looked down at her hands and realized she was holding them the whole time. Yvette had set up a lifestyle of giving her keys away that having them had become foreign to her. She had become used to someone in the driver seat of her life and she forgot that she no longer had to wait on anybody. She could make her own decisions. She allowed not only Jodi, but she continued to repeat the cycle of giving access to her old boyfriend that came out of prison to her apartment. He didn't ask. He just walked right in and set up residence where she once had access to walk freely all over her whole space. His presence became bigger than hers and she found herself confined to her bedroom as he tormented her mentally and even attempted to violate her in front of her son physically. So many of us have allowed a "Baby Boy" experience to take up residence and don't think that it always has to be a person to be in a Baby Boy's experience. Anything that you allow to rob you of your peace is your Baby Boy.

Understand this, just like a financial institution, God holds the title, but He gives us possession over the house. This means that we have the authority to evict anything that does not belong there. Despite the fact that at some point we welcomed them in. Realize that the house belongs to you. You have a right to take back your authority. It's time to say goodbye to some things in your life that are collecting dust, taking up too much space, are not useful, and causing you to vacate. One of the most infamous phrases many of us grew up hearing grown folks say is, "What goes on in this house stays in our house!" Well, that was a lie from the pit of hell because for some of us what went on in our house had been killing everything around us for too long. Everything can't stay in the house and we passed those things on to our children not knowing the weight of what that meant. To persevere, you have to make up your mind that some things have got to go before you. You don't need anyone's permission to change the locks and serve notice.

Taking Back Your Power

Sistah it's okay, get you a good therapist!

Women, especially African American women, for centuries ignore mental health issues. It was a taboo subject among black women, passed down from generation to generation as having "bad nerves" masking depression, staying busy, overeating or even forgetting to eat, and normalizing those behaviors as it kills slowly. Not only do Black women continue to have higher rates of physical illness with poorer quality of care, but we also experience higher rates of depression than our White counterparts. We are more likely to refuse to receive mental health treatment because many women still choose busyness. The upside is, as national attention shines a spotlight on mental health, Black women are slowly joining the discussions and the efforts to heal. A professional can help you by listening with a non-bias perspective, which can provide you with a different perspective on life.

The Need for Deliverance

So you've done some things. You made some choices that weren't thought or prayed out, but it felt right. We must be careful of depending on our feelings when in a place of vulnerability. It's not the best time to make decisions other than the decision to ask God for help.

If you choose not to, you may find yourself trapped in the closet of darkness, and the feelings of being stuck can begin to play on your need to do something, anything to get yourself out of this place. This dark closet will open itself up to what it's attracted to, which is more darkness. You can drink it, sex it, pill pop it, party it, overwork it, cry it, sing it, lie it, gym it, dress it up and call it pretty, and even church it away, but until you ask God for help, until you ask God to deliver you from these things that we use to cover the pain, you will only go deeper into that closet. However, there is Good News. God's deliverance can bring you out.

Above all else, with healing comes the need for deliverance. If you can push past that feeling of guilt and shame, be brave enough and not ashamed to call the pain out by its name. In God you can find safety. He is a safe place to be vulnerable. One of the most freeing feelings is to admit the truth. You will find peace by repenting, surrendering to God, and asking Him to deliver you.

Only then did I begin to feel worthy of having my keys, because I was now hearing the voice of God and believing that I could fight strongholds through God's deliverance. True deliverance will require an intentional effort on your part. It will require you to seek God. Not just daily but minute by minute. You will have to completely resist any and everything that doesn't look like the change you desire to see. If you know you're struggling with drinking, it wouldn't be wise to go to a bar. You have to treat deliverance the same way. You must stay away from things that tempt you back to toxic behaviors. It is a process, and some days it will feel like it would be easier to just stay toxic. If you seek God's guidance like never before, when you do, things have no choice but to change. Stay the course because the Bible declares that if you resist the devil, He will flee! Anything that takes up residence in our lives that we know isn't good for us yet find it difficult to release requires deliverance.

Stand on Your Deliverance

Now, this is the part where it can become frustrating and difficult. This is where the enemy shows up to convince you that you have not been saved by grace and delivered at all. He, in fact, will come at you harder and tempting you to go back to old habits or open that door back up to the same stuff you kicked out. It'll tempt you in the same way with a new face. But stay the course and stand on your deliverance!

After that, you purge people and things from your life that do not support a healthy and holistic lifestyle.

- Ask God to send you an accountability partner/prayer partner. You will need someone in your life that knows your struggle, won't judge your struggle, but will hold you to the standard that you are trying to live.

I keep a song in my heart that declares my deliverance:

"Never Be Bound Again" by Bishop Paul Morton

Your heart needs people constantly pouring into you and you need to be pouring into people. There's a constant flow coming in and out as you love and serve others. People need to hear about Jesus, and you need to grow in the Lord with your family that you'll be with for all eternity.

There will be times that you don't feel the Lord's presence or feel like He is listening to your prayers. Persevere! Trust that He is always completing a good work in you. Believe that the Lord will prevail in all things. As you persevere, you will continue to grow in Godliness and your heart will be strong.

Chapter 7

Strong Bonds

I have been blessed beyond measure to connect in one lifetime to so many phenomenal women. I know that God has given me the assignment to serve and impact the lives of women. On both my father and mother's side of the family, I have been in the presence of so many beautiful and intelligent women.

My mother was my teacher of life. She would always give me little nuggets of wisdom for me to hold on to. She was the first person who told me about Sojourner Truth and made me conscious of my thick, rich black culture. She preached modesty as a young woman, family and education. These were most important to her. My grandmother, Savannah, rest her soul, taught me about Jesus. She was the first person to tell me, as a child, that I would one day be saved. She would say that to me a lot, even when I didn't know what it meant. I am now saved, and I am crystal clear of what it means. Thank you, Grandma, for speaking that into my life.

My Grandma, "Dot" as I affectionately call her, is the richest color of chocolate and beautiful in spirit. I can call her to this day, and she would say, "Hunny! Don't you worry yo 'self, just give it to Jesus!" I love her for that. I have a host of aunties with colorful personalities that I am able to grab a little bit of this and a little bit of that from; style, grace, stance, volume, elegance, strength, take no mess, and quietness.

My two sisters are uniquely different, yet we mirror each other when we look at our children. We always rally together when we need to while knowing there is always love and respect for one another.

With a diploma in one hand and a pregnancy test in the other, my first born Khadijra, with her quiet, yet strong demeanor and bold hair taught me how to love something deeper than myself and was my first real responsibility. She embodies confidence and deep-rooted style that awakens a room like a sunflower. I appreciate her because she helps with grounding me in purpose. When I carried her, I had daydreams of what I hoped she'd become, and she has made those dreams come true.

My second born, Erickah, talked and walked at 6 months. She is bright, talkative, and a light to this world. She has a glow that the world will always try to put out, but she keeps shining. She is a fighter, compassionate and sweet. I love that about her. African Proverbs says a child born on Sunday is blessed, and what a beautiful Father's Day gift she was.

My youngest, Indyah, was in so many ways a saving grace. She came into this world looking around the room as if to say, "Where are my clothes? I'm here!" She is strong-minded, alert, and determined to dance to the beat of her own drum. She has eyes that hold the windows to her beautiful soul. She is a caregiver by nature and one day the world will appreciate every gift God has placed inside of her. We have formed bonds from their birth, but it's important for them to form their own as I did in this lifetime in order to be the woman that will impact another for the better.

More than anything, I felt the natural pulling on me to instill a sense of empowerment in my daughters. It is my responsibility to let them know early on that they can do anything they set their minds to. Whether it's your daughters, nieces, granddaughters, cousins, the little girl in your classroom, on the bus or at the grocery store, speaking greatness into them helps us all to create a new generation of women who will stop at nothing to achieve their dreams, while supporting and encouraging others to do the same.

Women are powerful not only in God, but in the world when we show our ability to form strong bonds amongst each other. We are most times, in house, on our jobs and in our churches, the glue that keeps us together. There have been so many wonderful women God sent to guide me on this journey called life and I am blessed to have made even the smallest connection with them. However, as much positivity we are able to exude, we must also recognize the deficiency that continues to keep us as a society of women divided. I know the weight of having been disconnected and the non-support of other women. It is very prevalent amongst us, alive and well.

So, why is it so hard for some women (myself very much included) to foster and gain positive, long-term relationships with each other? It seems like this was set in place long before many of us were born. I suspect this deficiency dates back historically to slavery, in which slaves as a whole were forcibly pitted against one another; particularly black women. The paper bag test was in full effect. This was when lighter complexioned mothers, daughters, and sisters were given an unfair, unjust advantage over so-called "darkies" jezebels, mammies, and jigaboos. This mindset breeds prejudices that continue to stain and cripple black women and relationships with each other to this day.

It has always disheartened me that women are each other's biggest and worst critics. We are the quickest to bring each other down, find each other's faults and nit-pick at a sister until she has nothing left, and nothing left to give. Then we step over her and call her worthless. We take the prettiest women and tear them down for 'thinking they're too cute' but turn around and dog the Sistah we view as average because 'we feel she should take better care of herself. We call strong women with strong personalities and a little education under her belt female dogs and accuse women who are sensitive of being weak as we throw them off to a man to care for them. Only because we find them useless to stand on their own. Then, we get jealous because she has a man!

We're quick to tear down a larger size woman if we see her overeating and criticize a skinny woman for not eating enough. We want the loud mouth, bossy Sistah to shut up for talking too much and turn around and bully the quiet, timid-looking woman for not taking up for herself. Another woman can't shout too much and pray too much or she's fake, but if she doesn't shout enough, her faith is under question. We withhold support of each other's businesses and throw each other under busses in boardrooms while sneaking around with other women's husbands in the bedroom. Sometimes, we can't win with each other! It's not that we can't win with each other. Often times, the issue could be that we don't feel that we're winning within. We possibly observed something in another woman that we desire for ourselves. We see something special in her that we just don't see in ourselves, and because we fail to grow up in that area, we turn that self-hate outward. This destructive pattern of abuse is crippling to our growth and development, and to our society as a whole.

I know there are women reading this very book who can relate. As women, we are good at dressing up our mess. We often cover up low self-esteem with a new comforter and pillow for the bed that we haven't even washed the sheets. We will buy a new rug without picking up the old one. But if we pulled back that comforter or pulled back the rug, we would see trash and dust that have collected for years because nobody cleaned it up. We can't effectively build someone else's house until we clean out our own. Too many women fall for the idea that in this heavily masculine, ambition driven society, in order to succeed, you have to suppress the feminine energy just to get things done, while managing not to get called the *B word for her strength. So many times, what they truly want to experience, which is love, goes neglected.

That's why it's so important to never judge another woman. The truth of the matter is that we have no idea what the next woman is going through. You don't know what past or current hurt and pains have shaped her into who she is today. If we would spend a fraction of the time building her up, instead of perpetuating what the world has written her off to be, just imagine how strong the bonds would be between mothers and daughters, sisters, aunties and anyone you pass. If we showed love, we could truly make a difference. The woman who walked into in my shoe store after going through chemo needed to be encouraged by another woman who knew the importance of being sensitive about her hair loss or breasts. The woman who lost her job and had to rely on public assistance for the first time needed her confidence back by being encouraged by another woman who wouldn't judge or look down on her. Encouragement to one another is not only important. It's vital for growth and development. When encouragement is absent from your life, you will begin to feel unloved, unimportant, useless, and forgotten. Many women will live this way without saying a word but act it out on others daily when all they really need is someone to look beyond their faults and speak to their needs. Every woman needs to be encouraged.

God commands that His people encourage each other because He knows we need it. In the Gospel of John, Jesus warned, "In this world, you will have trouble," which He then followed with a much-needed encouragement: "But take heart; I have overcome the world." (John 16:33)

I'm not suggesting that everyone will like one another because some personalities will clash. However, we can still walk in love with one another and we can all try to respect one another's differences, weaknesses, and strengths. Many times, the woman we're resisting is the one we could be learning from. The art of observation is for the wise woman who knows that if she keeps her eyes on what she wants, she will begin to manifest that thing in her own life. I can't tell you how many women I sat back and observed how they carried themselves. I watched their style, the way they paid their bills, how they budgeted their money, how they spoke to their husbands when they didn't agree with them, how they prayed about things they believed God for and how they behaved in public and in private. I studied how they stayed away from gossiping or how they dove right in for all the tea. I just learned the art of observation, and that helped me decide the course of what I could take away or throw away from other women. There is always something positive we can take away if we're intentional about building people up. Every woman can use a mentor in her life that can give good counsel and one that she can ask questions freely and just listen. Growing up, I remember how important it was to receive wisdom and guidance from the elders in my family and community. God was so gracious to send a woman in every space in life I have occupied. I've always been grateful for that. They were never afraid to both challenge and accept me. They helped build my confidence in which God said I am. When you do that, you invite grace in your life. There's a beauty and radiance that shows all over you when you live under God's grace. It is a peace, not arrogance. There's confidence in knowing that God's love can cover the areas you find difficult to love about yourself.

Breaking the Bond of Jealousy and Envy

- Taking ownership of the feelings of jealousy and envy will help you recognize that you will need to decide what kind of woman you are going to be to another woman. Ask yourself, "Am I going to be the backstabbing friendly enemy or the supportive confidant?"

There are only two choices. It's either to do well or to set out to do evil. You get to decide.

- Be willing to acknowledge it with the person who you are struggling with in that area. Ask for patience and support from her. This will call for your pride to be put completely aside and walk in full humility. (Pray and ask God for strength.)

- Be intentional about being happy for others. It's essential to learn to celebrate the victories of others if we are to proceed with the right heart so that we can walk in a place of favor. Refusing to rejoice for others blocks your blessings.

- Give meaningful compliments to other women. Identify a good quality in another woman. Zone in and let her know you noticed it. You have no idea whether that compliment was just what they needed and you're teaching them to pay it forward.

- Pray and ask God to deliver you from this type of stronghold. The more you walk in love with others and command that spirit to leave you, the stronger you become as you weaken its grip.

- Stay away from gossip. They breed negativity and keep the dysfunctional and abusive cycle of jealousy going.

The fact of the matter is, we need one another. Helping one woman helps all women. It's our nature and brings out the best in all of us. We can only create an atmosphere of love that we long for from each other by tightening our bonds. Most of all, be the change you want to see.

To every woman reading this, I love you, and let me be the first to say I'm sorry if I've ever hurt or offended you. If my tone was sharp and arrogant, if I've ever made you feel less than what I know your greatness is, if I failed to show support to you, please forgive me. I ask that you join me in becoming more intentional about the way we as women show love to one another. There are young girls that precede us, and they need us to set the example for them. They watch how we handle one another, and we must do better to handle each other with care because they too will need to be handled with care. Please, partner with me in prayer as we plead the blood over the spirit of pettiness, strife, low self-esteem, self-righteousness, pride, envy, and jealous behaviors. Let's reconnect and stay connected through the grace that God has shown us in spite of us.

My Sistah, your house was established and built by God, and it is not anyone's place to break in and tear it down. I stand in solitude to every dream birthed in you and there is no level of melanin that can break our bond ever again.

Chapter 8

Living Under Grace

I had heard so many times people talking about having grace and mercy, but it took me awhile to know the difference between the two and the understanding that I would need both. Mercy withholds a punishment we deserve but grace gives us a gift of blessings we don't deserve. Either way, we are so undeserving, but God does it anyway.

I grew up hearing the women, particularly my grandmother, saying Lord have mercy when things would happen that she didn't have answers for. Mercy would always be what she would ask for. I heard this phrase so much that it wasn't until later in life that I learned about the power of grace. Don't get me wrong, I've messed up many prayers by asking God for grace when what I really needed was mercy. I needed God to forgive me for things that didn't please him about me. I needed mercy for all the times I didn't forgive others when I, myself, had received forgiveness freely. That was an act of mercy.

Every day that we live is an act of God's mercy. If God gave us all what we deserved, we would all be in line headed to hell. We spend a lifetime of lying, backstabbing, cheating, stealing, killing, and the ways we choose to treat our fellow neighbor here on earth while we love all things less important would certainly be our ticket in.

How many times have you cried out "Lord have mercy" over something that you know if God didn't fix, remove, shift, or transform, it wouldn't get done and you I would still be a mess? Let's talk about those things that didn't go the way you had hoped for or you may have set out to prepare for yourself that you wanted to achieve. Because you wanted it so bad, you didn't wait to hear from God. You stepped out on blind faith anyway. While things seemed to be going well for a while and then BOOM! Everything you worked hard for just fell completely apart. As you saw it crumbling, the first thing that crossed your mind was whether God gave you permission? And you can't seem to recall. Well this is certainly a "Lord have mercy on me" moment.

While the Bible often talks about mercy as it relates to our sins, that isn't always the case. At times, we can have mercy (or receive it) in situations of trial or discomfort and we have needed it to overcome. You cannot truly overcome sin unless God gives you both mercy and grace. The truth of the matter is that you need mercy to forgive others, maybe even yourself and you need grace to go on. God shows us both mercy and grace, but they are not the same. In mercy, God chose to cancel our sin debt by sacrificing His perfect Son in our place. The Bible states it, and I have lived it that we have all sinned and fell short of God's glory, fell short of pleasing God and obeying what He clearly asked us to do. We all deserve death and eternal judgment in the lake of fire. I never thought about how deep that really is and we often take what has been extended to us for granted. Mercy and grace are best shown through the salvation that was given to us by Jesus Christ.

The Good News is that you get to exercise grace and mercy in your life right now. We are all still being built daily. So in the same manner He is still building us, we should try and build others up by extending the same level of mercy and grace to others. You can't talk about overcoming unless you talk about this important word, forgiveness. Forgiveness is the key that unlocks the door, and unforgiveness robs us of God's favor. When we tap into his power within, we get the strength to break free from harboring unforgiveness. I encourage you to walk boldly and confidently in the Lord, knowing that with His grace and mercy, you can be free of what didn't go right and begin to walk in love. Then the outpouring of grace will move in your direction.

Matthew 11:28 says *"Come to me, all you who are weary and burdened, and I will give you rest."* As we walk in God's love and grace, His favor is released, and you'll be introduced to a newfound freedom. When I felt grace over my life, it wasn't that everything was in order, but favor followed me. When I needed gas money, someone would walk up to me and place a twenty-dollar bill in my hand without knowing that was my need. When I was low on food, my daughters and I got an invite out to dinner. I began to appreciate grace however and whenever it decided to show up.

To truly appreciate grace you have to rest on God's promises because it forces worry to cease its activity and give you another reason to trust in Him even more. If there's ever a time where you are faced with trials, rest on knowing that His promises will do a work in you while you wear His grace as a covering. While wearing His garment of grace, we receive His peace, protection, and provision. You will need His strength to renew your mind and heal your heart from whatever has caused damage. Discipline yourself to get quiet and hear more than talking and trust that He is working things out for you. If you truly want to move forward, giving up your way and yielding to His is the only way and you must see it that way. The reality is, you can't do it by yourself anyway.

2 Corinthians 12:9 *"But He said to me, "My grace is sufficient for you, for my power is made perfect in weakness." Therefore I will boast all the more gladly of my weaknesses, so that the power of Christ may rest upon me."*

If you are like me, I'm sure you're happy that you don't look like all that you've been through. It's a blessing to know that we have a Father who cares about us so much that He wants us to live the abundant life, full of hope and promise.

We often miss out on the blessing because we don't believe deep down in our hearts that type of life is for us. We must be willing to receive and embrace all that God has for us even if we feel we don't deserve it. There's an unmerited favor when we allow His grace over our life and you'll know when you don't have it. I wouldn't suggest stepping outside of His will to find out either! Whatever you do, stay in His will or His way. Either way, don't leave His presence because it's not guaranteed that grace will follow you.

He truly is the only one that can transform the pains of past and present to purpose. I'm sure as long as we live and God continues to operate His power in us, we will still face some stress-filled challenging days that will require you and I to revisit every chapter of this book to keep on going. From the beauty from learning about the power of God, I've learned that His power keeps working long after my flesh tires out. I've learned that even when I have to face challenges, all I have to do is remember who was the architect that builds me and what's inside me. The very thought strengthens me to keep going when life says to stop right here. In addition, the reward for not giving up is grace waiting to redeem the time wasted, lost or stolen, grace to give your joy back, and the restoration of hope. The covering of grace is beautiful and evident to others who are watching you to see how you are getting through in the face of adversity. Ask for God's mercy when you need it but to be overcome with purpose, pray for His grace.

In this season, I encourage you to tap into the power that lives in you. It's there waiting on you to activate it. When you do, you will be ready to experience living a life not void of problems but one full of promise. You will be able to thrive. While it may appear things are falling apart, you will still be standing.

It is my prayer that you be empowered with God's strength and peace as it sustains you as you forget the former things of your past and move forward reaching for the things that are ahead. I can assure you that if you activate and trust the power of the Holy Spirit by allowing it to take up permanent residence in your house, you'll discover that the person you've always wanted to be is who you truly are. No matter what comes your way, with the Holy Spirit inside, it will have to break before it breaks you!

Now, What's In Your House?

Enjoy these Writing Prompts to begin your Journaling Experience....

1. Dear God, it weighs on me that I never confess to you that I....

   _____

   _____

   _____

2. The feeling I got when I removed myself from a situation that robbed my house of peace...

   _____

   _____

   _____

3. The biggest lie I've ever told myself was ...

   _____

   _____

   _____

4. Is there anything you feel guilty about? Is there anything you need to be forgiven for?

   _____

   _____

   _____

5. *What's the worst thing you've ever done?*

_____

_____

_____

6. *What's your secret desire?*

_____

_____

_____

7. *What's the most outrageous thing you've ever done?*

_____

_____

_____

8. *My favorite way to spend the day is...*

_____

_____

_____

9. *If I could talk to my younger self at age 8, 18 and 28, I would say is ....*

_____

_____

_____

10. The two moments I'll never forget in my life are...
Describe them in great detail, and what makes them
so unforgettable.

_____

_____

_____

11. When I'm in pain — physical or emotional — the
kindest thing I can do for myself is...

_____

_____

_____

12. Make a list of the people in your life who genuinely
support you, and who you can genuinely trust. (Then
make time to hang out with them)

_____

_____

_____

13. *What does unconditional love look like for you?*

_____

_____

_____

14. *What would you do if you loved yourself unconditionally? How can you act on these things whether you do or don't?*

_____

_____

_____

15. *I really wish others knew this about me...*

_____

_____

_____

16. *Name what is **enough** for you?*

_____

_____

_____

17. What are you grateful for?

_____

_____

_____

18. Have you honored every room in your house? Have
you furnished it with love or is it some place still
empty and need help?

_____

_____

_____

About Arifah N. Goodwin

Arifah N. Goodwin is a wife, a mother, and a woman of God. As an inspirational speaker, minister, author, and entrepreneur, she is passionate about empowerment of others, and serving her community. Her goal in life is simple: To do whatever God calls her to do, hopefully inspiring others to do the same.

For Booking Inquiries & Speaking Engagements, contact:

Website: www.GoodEmpowers.com

Email: ArifahGoodwinEmpowers@gmail.com

Facebook: Arifah Empowers

Let's stay connected on Facebook, and also feel free to leave me a book review on Amazon.com. I appreciate your support!

The Power to Overcome is in You!

Made in the USA
Middletown, DE
25 July 2022